donna hay

SIMPLE ESSENTIALS

beef, lamb + pork

thank you

I have so many people to thank for helping with this book: Vanessa Pitsikas, for being a designer wise, composed and talented beyond her years; food editors Justine Poole, Steve Pearce and Jane Collings and their dedicated team of recipe testers for dishes that elicit oohs and aahs every time; copy editor Kirsty McKenzie for always asking the right questions; the amazing Con Poulos, talented Chris Court and all the other photographers whose images shine on every page; and, of course, to the *donna hay magazine* staff for being all-round superstars – your loyalty, creativity and professionalism help make donna hay a truly world-class brand. Many thanks must also be extended to Phil Barker at News Magazines; and to the team at HarperCollins. Thank you, thank you to friends old and new and my dear family. And to the men in my life: my wonderful sons Angus and Tom who make my heart soar, and my partner, Bill.

on the cover
front: lamb cutlets with tarragon-potato salad, page 50
back: red wine and beef simmer, page 34

Fourth Estate

An imprint of HarperCollins*Publishers*

First published in Australia and New Zealand in 2008,
by Fourth Estate, an imprint of HarperCollins*Publishers*
HarperCollins*Publishers* Australia Pty Limited
25 Ryde Road, Pymble, Sydney, NSW 2073, Australia
ABN 36 009 913 517

HarperCollins*Publishers*
31 View Road, Glenfield, Auckland 10, New Zealand

Copyright © Donna Hay 2008. Design copyright © Donna Hay 2008
Photographs copyright © Con Poulos 2008 pages 4, 7, 9, 10, 11, 12, 13, 14, 15, 17, 20, 22 (left), 23, 24, 25, 29 (right), 31, 32 (left), 35, 37 (right), 40, 41, 45 (right), 47, 52 (left), 55, 56, 57 (left), 59, 60 (left), 61, 63, 65, 67, 68, 69 (left), 71, 72 (right), 75, 76, 77, 79, 80 (left), 94, 96, back cover; copyright © Chris Court cover, pages 1, 18, 19, 21, 28, 29 (left), 33, 36, 37 (left), 43, 45 (left), 48, 49, 51, 52 (right), 53, 60 (right), 69 (right), 72 (left), 73, 80 (right), 81, 83, 85, 87; copyright © Ben Dearnley pages 32 (right), 57 (right); copyright © Amanda McLauchlan pages 16, 39; copyright © Brett Stevens pages 22 (right), 27.

Food Editors: Justine Poole, Steve Pearce, Jane Collings
Styling: Donna Hay, Justine Poole, Steve Pearce, Clara Luboff
Recipe testing: Miranda Farr
Designer: Vanessa Pitsikas
Copy Editor: Kirsty McKenzie
Consulting Art Director: Sarah Kavanagh

Reproduction by Graphic Print Group, South Australia
Produced in Hong Kong by Phoenix Offset on 157gsm Chinese Matt Art.
Printed in China.

National Library of Australia Cataloguing-in-Publication data:
Hay, Donna.
Beef, lamb and pork.
Includes index.
ISBN 978 0 7322 8582 1 (hbk.).
1. Cookery (Beef). 2. Cookery (Lamb). 3. Cookery (Pork).
I. Title. (Series : Simple essentials).
641.36

08 09 10 11   10 9 8 7 6 5 4 3

donna hay

SIMPLE ESSENTIALS

beef, lamb + pork

FOURTH ESTATE

contents

introduction

As my guiding principle in the kitchen is always to buy the best produce available, that means I'm prepared to go to considerable effort to source best cuts of meat. I actually met my husband, Bill, when I was on the hunt for the perfect leg of lamb for a photo shoot. I found the lamb and the man of my dreams so I guess you could say that was a successful mission. A farmer and a butcher, Bill's favourite roast is actually a lamb shoulder. But that requires the luxury of time for the slow cooking to ensure the sweet meat literally falls off the bone. This collection of recipes has a few of those weekend treats for your family and friends but we've also included loads of lamb, beef and pork recipes for everyday occasions when you need simple flavour-packed dishes that are quick to prepare. I'm sure some of them will become your trusted stand-bys.

Donna

basics

Ever wished you had a butcher on call to help you as you select, prepare and cook beef, lamb and pork? This comprehensive chapter could be the answer to your prayers as it guides you through the most popular cuts and cooking methods. There are also expert tips for achieving perfect results every time and recipes for your favourite accompaniments and sauces.

all about beef

When you need meat that is packed with flavour and simple to prepare, beef is an obvious choice. This guide to cuts and cooking styles will make sure every dish turns out just as you've planned.

scotch fillet

Cut from the rib section of the beef forequarter, the scotch fillet, also known as the rib fillet or the rib eye steak, is one of the most tender and flavoursome cuts. As a whole piece, also known as a cube roll, it can be roasted at 200°C (400°F). A rack of scotch fillet with the bone in forms that English dinner table classic, the standing, or prime, rib roast. Steaks, with or without the bone attached, should be pan-fried or char-grilled (broiled) from medium-rare to medium to preserve maximum juiciness and tenderness.

rump + topside

From the hindquarter of the beast, the rump (top and centre) provides great steaks for char-grilling (broiling) and pan-frying. Whole rumps can be roasted at 200°C (400°F). The outer fat layer provides a good inbuilt self-basting device, which can easily be trimmed after cooking. Topside steak (bottom of pic) is an adjoining cut, which can also be grilled, but requires marinating and basting to keep it moist. It can also be cut into strips for stir-frying, or roasted at 160°C (320°F) with frequent basting to stop it drying out.

eye + butt fillet

The most tender (and expensive) steak comes from the beef tenderloin. The eye fillet (left) tapers from a thin point to a section of uniform width sold variously as fillet steak, beef tournedos, filet mignon and eye fillet. The thicker end (right) is sold as butt fillet, another premium cut for grilling and roasting. These lean cuts should be seared to enhance colour and flavour before roasting at 200°C (400°F). Baste during cooking. As steaks, they should be char-grilled (broiled) rare to medium. Overcooking will toughen them.

sirloin + T-bone

The striploin yields the sirloin which is a great cut for slow roasting as a whole piece or char-grilling (broiling) as steaks. The sirloin is also sometimes sold as New York steak. Whole sirloin (top) can be roasted at 160°C (320°F) with the fat side up, to baste as it cooks. When char-grilling (broiling) sirloin steaks, sear to brown then baste during cooking. The T-bone (left) has the bone in, with the striploin (sirloin) on one side of the bone and the tenderloin (eye fillet) on the other. Porterhouse steak is similar, though with more tenderloin.

round, blade + chuck

Clockwise from top: round, blade and chuck steaks are the sweethearts of the slow-cook set. Round and blade can be grilled (broiled), but they benefit from marinating and basting. They can also be sliced thinly and pounded into minute steaks for sandwiches. These cuts also respond well to crumbing, which seals in the juices, tenderising as it cooks. Cut into strips for stir-fries, dice for stews or braises, or pot-roast whole with plenty of liquid and vegies. Chuck is the true slow-cook hero, ideal for curries, braises and stews.

beef shin

Cut from the leg, beef shin, shank or gravy beef as it is sometimes labelled, is sold both with the bone in and boned. Its high gelatine content makes it ideal for slow cooking in stock or other braising liquid, but care should be taken not to overcook, as the meat will fall apart. It should be trimmed of all visible fat and sinew before cooking. The same cut from a young calf is sold as veal osso bucco. Because it's young, it's leaner and more tender than beef shin and requires less cooking time. It also has a more delicate flavour.

all about lamb

If you're looking for meat that is sweet, tender and moist, you can't go past lamb. Use this guide to help you choose the right cut and cooking method to ensure optimum results every time.

leg + easy-carve

Lamb leg with the bone in is the classic roast, best trimmed of excess fat before placing in the oven at 180°C (350°F). Baste with pan juices during cooking to keep moist. Avoid overcooking to maintain tenderness and juiciness. Rest the lamb before carving, to ensure the meat is moist and tender. The easy-carve roast has most of the bone removed but the shank bone is retained, providing a convenient handle for carving. They're also easy to stuff and need less roasting time than legs with the bone in, so they're great for busy cooks.

rack + cutlets

The rack of lamb has anywhere between four and 12 ribs and is a great cut for roasting at 200°C (400°C). Baste often during the short roasting time, or spread with mustard and/or herbs and breadcrumbs to seal in the juices. Cutlets are simply lamb racks cut into individual chops. Char-grill (broil) or pan-fry for a couple of minutes each side. They should not be cooked from extremely cold as the meat will become tough. Lamb cutlets or racks described as French-trimmed or Frenched have all visible fat removed.

backstrap + fillet

Technically the eye muscle of the shortloin, the lamb backstrap (boneless loin) (left) is a tender and versatile cut that responds well to being barbecued, pan-fried or char-grilled (broiled) and cut into strips for stir-frying. It responds well to brief cooking and resting before slicing. Take care not to overcook as the meat can become tough and dry. The same advice applies to the lamb tenderloin or fillet (right). Perhaps the most failsafe of all lamb cuts, it can be barbecued, pan-fried, char-grilled (broiled) or stir-fried in strips.

boneless loin + chops

The loin of the lamb yields a range of cuts that can be roasted and pan-fried or char-grilled (broiled). A whole, boned, rolled loin (left) should be roasted at 180°C (350°F). When sliced into portions, this cut is sometimes described as a lamb noisette. The loin with the bone is also a popular roasting cut, though not as easy to carve as the boned version. Roast at 200°C (400°F). When sliced into individual servings, this cut delivers loin chops, best pan-fried or char-grilled (broiled) and served medium-rare.

leg steaks

Steaks cut from the leg of lamb (left) are great for pan-frying or char-grilling (broiling). They are sold both with the bone in and boned. Either pound lightly to tenderise or marinate and baste frequently to add flavour to the meat while cooking. Lamb rump steaks (right) are portions cut from the leg section known as the chump. The ones in this photograph have been trimmed of all visible fat and gristle. The untrimmed versions are sold as chump chops. Whole lamb rumps can also be pot-roasted.

shoulder + shanks

Most commonly sold boned and rolled as a roast to be seasoned or stuffed and cooked at 180°C (350°F), the shoulder with the bone in is also a brilliant cut for long, slow roasting at 160°C (320°F). Trim the joint of all visible fat, add plenty of stock and wine or balsamic vinegar to the pot, then cover and let the oven work its magic. Lamb shanks also respond well to long, slow cooking. Ask your butcher to French, or trim, both ends of the shanks; although not essential, it makes handling easier and they fit better in the pan.

all about pork

Many cooks steer away from pork because they think it's difficult to cook. In fact, by selecting the right cuts and not overcooking them, you'll end up with the most succulent meat every time.

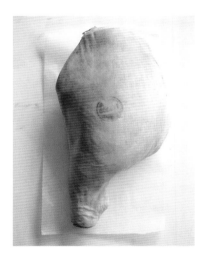

leg roast

A perfectly cooked leg of pork with a crispy layer of crackling is truly one of life's great privileges. Make sure the rind is dry before you score it with a sharp knife, smear it with oil and rub with salt. Roast at 220°C (430°F) for 20 minutes. Reduce the heat to 180°C (350°F) and roast for 20 minutes per 500g (1 lb) for legs of less than 3kg (6¾ lb) weight and 15 minutes per 500g (1 lb) for legs weighing more than 3kg (6¾ lb). Rest the leg after roasting, as this allows the fibres to relax and ensures the meat is tender.

rolled loin + rack

The loin yields some of the best roasting meat as it has that all-important layer of fat enclosing a lean interior. Racks with the bone in are great for portion control as you can serve one rib per guest. To roast a rolled loin (left) cook for 20 minutes at 220°C (430°F), then reduce heat and cook for a further 45 minutes per kg (2¼ lb) at 180°C (350°F). Times for a pork rack (centre) are the same, but for a trimmed, partially boned rack (right) there is no need for the initial high heat. Roast at 180°C (350°F) for 45 minutes per kg (2¼ lb).

fillet

The question isn't what can you do with pork fillet, but what can't you do. Stir-fried with noodles, roasted in the oven with vegies, glazed for kebabs on the barbecue, seared and cooked on the barbecue, or pan-fried with a creamy mustard sauce, the fillet or tenderloin is one of the most adaptable of pork cuts. It's also the leanest with less fat than chicken breast and twice the amount of iron. Baste frequently during cooking or wrap in prosciutto or bacon to maintain juiciness. Roast at 180°C (350°F) for 20 minutes per 300g (10½ oz).

loin chops + cutlets

The juiciest (and therefore most popular) grilling cut is the pork loin chop (left) which has a lovely outer fat layer enclosing a lean interior. It should be barbecued, pan-fried or char-grilled (broiled) for 3–5 minutes each side, depending on the thickness of the chop. Pork cutlets (right) are cut from the mid-loin and trimmed of all visible fat, making them popular with people who are watching fat counts. Because cutlets are so lean, they need brushing with oil before being barbecued, pan-fried or char-grilled (broiled) for 3–5 minutes each side.

butterfly steaks

Steaks cut from the loin are often sold butterflied, that is, cut almost in half so they can be opened out, to speed up cooking time and increase the surface area for take up of marinades or sauces. Cooking times are brief – no more than 3–5 minutes each side, depending on the thickness of the steak – to ensure the meat stays juicy and tender. Butterfly steaks tend to have most of the visible fat removed, so a light brushing with oil is recommended before char-grilling (broiling), barbecuing or pan-frying.

ribs + belly

Succulent pork belly, with its alternating layers of fat and meat, long an Asian delicacy, is now a universal favourite when slow-roasted to melting tenderness. Belly can be braised in a soy master stock for spectacular effect. When cut into strips, belly pork becomes spare ribs which can be barbecued, pan-fried or char-grilled (broiled) or roasted at 190°C (375°F) for 50 minutes per 500g (1 lb). American style ribs are leaner, usually roasted in slabs and brushed with a marinade. Cooking times are the same as for spare ribs.

roasting beef

Roast beef is an all-time favourite. The succulent meat and much-loved trimmings are utterly irresistible. Better still, it's surprisingly simple to prepare and speedy to cook.

ready to roast

Preheat the oven to 220°C (430°F). Sprinkle salt and generous amounts of freshly cracked pepper onto a piece of baking paper. Brush the beef with olive oil and roll it in the salt and pepper, pressing firmly until the meat is well coated. Tie with kitchen string to help the meat keep its shape. Wrap the string around the meat and tie knots at 4cm (1½ in) intervals along the length of the beef. Always use proper kitchen string. Other string is often plastic-coated and could burn or melt and give the beef a chemical taint.

browning the meat

Before placing the meat in the oven, brown it in a non-stick frying pan over high heat to seal in the juices and prevent the meat from drying out while roasting. Searing or browning the meat also gives better appearance and flavour, particularly for smaller, high-temperature, fast-cooked boneless roasts. Heat a large non-stick frying pan over high heat. Cook the beef for 1–2 minutes on each side or until browned. Choose a baking dish that's as close as possible to the size of the roast, to stop the pan juices evaporating or burning.

ruling the roast

Place the beef on a rack in a baking dish and roast in the preheated 220°C (430°F) oven for 15 minutes to continue the browning process. Reduce the temperature to 180°C (350°F) and continue roasting. Use the pan juices to baste the meat as it cooks – add a little stock, water or wine to the pan if there's not much juice. For every 500g (1 lb) of beef, cook for 15 minutes for rare and 20 minutes for medium. After roasting cover the meat with aluminium (aluminum) foil and let it rest in a warm place for 10–20 minutes.

roasting lamb

Crispy on the outside, juicy on the inside, lamb roast is everyone's favourite. From stuffing and tying to marinating, our guide shows you how to roast a leg of lamb to rival even your mum's.

before you begin

For a traditional roast lamb with rosemary and garlic you will need: 1 bone-in or easy-carve leg of trimmed lamb, 1 bunch rosemary, 2 halved heads garlic, olive oil for rubbing and sea salt. Preheat the oven to 180°C (350°F). The sides of the pan should not be too high, as the roast will not brown well. If it's too shallow the juices will splatter the oven. About 8cm (3¼ in) is ideal. To serve up to four people, you will need 1.75–2kg (3½–4 lb) leg of lamb; up to six people, 2–2.5kg (4–5 lb); up to eight people, more than 2.5kg (5 lb).

preparing the roast

Place the rosemary on the top of the leg and secure with kitchen string. A roasting rack in the pan allows the heat to circulate around the roast so it browns evenly. In this case the garlic does the job of the rack, so place the lamb on top of the halves. Rub the skin with oil and sprinkle with salt. Bake for the calculated cooking time or until cooked to your liking. Allow the roast to stand for 10–20 minutes before carving. To keep the succulent flavour and juiciness of roast lamb, it is best cooked until pink (medium).

roasting times

Weigh the lamb to determine the cooking time. Use the table below as a guide and increase or decrease the time if you prefer well-done or rare lamb.

Roasting times in preheated 180°C (350°F) oven to result in medium cooked meat.	
cut of lamb	time per 500g (1 lb)
traditional leg	18–20 min
butterflied leg	10 min
easy-carve leg	18–20 min
rump	10–12 min

17

roasting pork loin

Roast pork loin may be a Christmas classic, but once you've mastered
the basics of preparing and cooking it, your family and friends won't
let you wait until the festive season to serve it.

preparing the loin

To make room for the stuffing in a boneless
loin of pork, you need to use a sharp knife
to separate and cut away the small fillet
and any excess meat from around the loin.
(Retain the small fillet and pan-fry or add
to stir-fries.) Alternatively, ask your butcher
to do this for you. With the point of a sharp
knife, score the skin of the pork at 1.5cm
(⅔ in) intervals. Use the knife to separate
the skin from the loin, leaving 3cm (1¼ in)
joined. Place the stuffing down the middle.
Roll the loin over the stuffing and secure
by tying with kitchen string.

thyme + onion stuffing

Place 1 tablespoon oil and 125g (4 oz)
butter in a non-stick frying pan over medium
heat. Add 4 sliced onions and cook, stirring
occasionally, for 10–15 minutes or until soft
and golden. Remove from the heat and mix
in 2 tablespoons thyme leaves and 4 cups
(200g/7 oz) fresh breadcrumbs. This stuffing
can be varied by replacing the thyme and
onion with 2 cups chopped rocket (arugula)
and ¼ cup roasted pine nuts and reducing
the butter quantity to 80g (2¾ oz). Melt
the butter and combine with the fresh
breadcrumbs, rocket and nuts.

roast to perfection

Preheat the oven to 220°C (430°F). Rub
the skin with oil and salt. Place the meat
on a rack in a baking dish. Bake for
20 minutes. Reduce the heat to 200°C
(400°F) and bake for 25 minutes per
500g (1 lb), or until the pork is cooked
to your liking. Remove the string and slice.
It isn't necessary to cook pork until it is
completely dried out, as was the practice
in the past. Test with a metal skewer:
if the juices run nearly clear, the pork
is cooked sufficiently and will have
a slightly pink centre when carved.

the perfect steak

Keep it simple, follow these guidelines and with one quick turn of the tongs you'll find your steaks will be tender and juicy every time. Don't forget the golden rule to rest the steak before serving.

before you start

Chilled meat takes longer to cook and as you want to cook the steaks briefly to preserve their juiciness, it's best to take them from the fridge and stand them at room temperature for about 10 minutes before cooking. To serve four people you will need 4 x 220g (7¾ oz) steaks. Pat the steaks dry with absorbent paper. Brush or spray with olive oil and sprinkle evenly with sea salt and cracked black pepper. Do this just before cooking so the salt will not have time to draw out the juices, which would toughen the meat.

pan-frying

Heat a large frying pan over high heat. Add the steaks and cook for 3 minutes on each side for medium-rare or until cooked to your liking. Turn the steaks only once as with each turn you lose the juices that have collected on the surface of the steak. Remove from the pan and set aside for 5 minutes. It is extremely important to rest the meat to allow the fibres to relax and reabsorb juices to ensure maximum tenderness. This method can also be followed for char-grilling (broiling) and cooking steak on the barbecue.

testing for doneness

Don't cut into the steak to see if it is cooked to your taste. Learn to tell by pressing the steak with tongs or a spatula.

Use this table as a guide for cooking steak. Adjust times according to the thickness.

steak	time per side	touch test
rare	2 min	very soft
medium-rare	3 min	soft
medium	4 min	springy
medium-well	4½ min	firm
well done	5 min	very firm

prepping essentials

weight + time

Kitchen string helps roasts hold their shape during cooking. If you don't feel confident testing your roast with a skewer, a thermometer can be left in the joint while cooking. Once it reaches the right temperature the roast is ready. An oven thermometer will ensure your oven is running at the temperature recommended in the recipe to cook the meat evenly. Most recipes give roasting times per weight, so scales are an asset.

tying

Tying the meat keeps its shape during roasting, helps to cook it more evenly and keeps any additions to the roast, such as herbs, firmly in place during cooking. Begin tying by making a loop around the thickest end of the joint. Then, on the top side, tie the string at 4cm (1½ in) intervals along the meat. When you come to the end, turn it over and thread the string under the loops along the underside. Tie a firm knot to the front to finish.

perfect crackling

Place the unwrapped pork on a plate in the fridge until ready to prepare. This dries the skin dry out, which helps create a crunchy surface. Make sure the oven is very hot – preheat for about 20 minutes. Rub salt and oil into the scored pork after tying. Scoring makes carving easier and helps give the skin its crispiness. Use the point of a sharp knife to make indents into the skin about 3–5mm (⅛–¼ in) deep at 1½cm (⅔ in) intervals.

resting meat

All meats benefit from resting after roasting for at least 10 minutes. This allows the juices to redistribute in the meat, giving a moister and more tender result. It also makes carving easier. Transfer the roast to a plate or carving dish, cover loosely with aluminium (aluminum) foil and rest the roast in a warm place. Meanwhile, make use of any pan juices by adding stock or wine to the roasting pan and boiling until slightly reduced.

cooking essentials

chilli, cumin, fennel + sea salt rub

Place ½ teaspoon cumin seeds, ½ teaspoon black peppercorns, ½ teaspoon fennel seeds, 4 dried chillies, ½ teaspoon turmeric and 1 teaspoon of flaked sea salt in a mortar and pestle and grind until it forms a powder. Brush meat with olive oil and sprinkle with the chilli, cumin, fennel and salt rub. Meat is best cooked on the barbecue or pan-fried. This rub is a great complement for beef, lamb and pork.

balsamic + caper marinade

Combine ½ cup (125ml/4 fl oz) balsamic vinegar, ⅓ cup (80ml/2½ fl oz) olive oil, 1 tablespoon lemon juice, 4 sliced cloves garlic, 2 tablespoons rinsed and drained salted capers, 1 teaspoon sugar, 2 teaspoons sea salt flakes, 1 teaspoon cracked black pepper, 3 chopped rosemary sprigs and 3 extra rosemary sprigs in a large non-metallic bowl. Marinate lamb racks or cutlets before roasting, pan-frying or barbecuing.

sticky soy marinade

Place ¼ cup (60ml/2 fl oz) kecap manis (see glossary),
1 tablespoon honey, 2 tablespoons olive oil, 1 crushed clove
garlic, 1 teaspoon finely grated ginger, 2 star anise and cracked
black pepper in a bowl and stir well to combine. Place meat in
a dish and brush with the marinade. Barbecue, char-grill (broil),
pan-fry or roast meat until caramelised and cooked through.
This is a great marinade to use with lamb, beef and pork.

garlic, lemon + chilli wet rub

Place 1 finely chopped long red chilli, 2 crushed cloves garlic,
1 teaspoon finely grated lemon rind, 1 tablespoon lemon juice,
2 tablespoons olive oil and sea salt in a non-metallic bowl and
stir to combine. Place meat in a dish and pour the mixture over.
The meat can be barbecued, pan-fried, roasted or char-grilled
(broiled) until cooked to your liking. This rub is great to use with
beef, lamb and pork.

essential sides

gravy

Remove the roast from the dish; cover with foil to keep warm. Pour the pan juices into a jug, add ice cubes and allow the fat to solidify on the ice; discard the fatty ice. Place the now empty baking dish over medium heat. Add 2–3 tablespoons plain (all-purpose) flour and stir for 2–3 minutes or until the mixture turns golden. Add 2 cups (500ml/16 fl oz) stock or water, bring to the boil and stir for 3–4 minutes to thicken. Makes 2 cups.

béarnaise sauce

Place 100ml (3½ fl oz) white wine in a pan with 2 tablespoons white wine vinegar and 1½ tablespoons chopped tarragon. Cook over high heat for 5 minutes or until reduced to 2 tablespoons. Strain and place in a small clean saucepan. Add 3 egg yolks and whisk over low heat for 40–50 seconds or until thick; don't overcook or the eggs will scramble. Remove from the heat and gradually whisk in 125g (4 oz) melted butter. Makes ¾ cup.

apple + sage chutney

Peel, core and chop 6 apples, combine with 1 chopped onion, 1½ cups (330g/11½ oz) caster (superfine) sugar, 1½ cups (375ml/12 fl oz) cider vinegar, 1 cup (250ml/8 fl oz) water and 3 x 5cm pieces lemon rind in a saucepan over medium heat and stir until the sugar dissolves. Simmer for 20 minutes. Add ¾ cup sage leaves, sea salt and black pepper and cook for 15 minutes or until the apples are soft. Makes 4 cups.

mint sauce

Place 1 finely chopped eschalot, 1 cup (220g/7¾ oz) caster (superfine) sugar, ¾ cup (185ml/6 fl oz) water and ¼ cup (60ml/2 fl oz) malt vinegar in a small saucepan and stir over low heat until the sugar dissolves. Bring to the boil and simmer for 15 minutes or until thick and syrupy. Allow to cool. Add ¼ cup finely chopped mint leaves, 2 tablespoons extra malt vinegar, sea salt and cracked black pepper to the syrup. Makes 1½ cups.

beef

When the conversation turns to beef, it usually concentrates on the exceptional flavour. For cooking ease and speed it's hard to go past the prime cuts, which are best roasted or grilled. However, there are also plenty of rewards to be reaped from the slow-cooked lesser cuts. I hope this selection from my favourite beef recipes adds a new batch of signature dishes to your "best ever" list.

slow-cooked veal osso bucco

sirloin steak with red wine sauce

honey mustard beef stir-fry

slow-cooked veal osso bucco

¼ cup (60ml/2 fl oz) olive oil

4 x 200g (7 oz) veal osso buco

plain flour, for dusting

1 leek, chopped

2 cloves garlic, crushed

2 tablespoons tomato paste

½ cup (125ml/4 fl oz) red wine

¾ cup (185ml/6 fl oz) tomato puree

3 cups (750ml/ 24 fl oz) beef stock

2 sprigs rosemary

3 bay leaves

sea salt and cracked black pepper

400g (14 oz) can white (cannellini) beans, drained

Heat 2 tablespoons of the oil in a deep frying pan over medium heat. Dust the veal with flour and cook for 3–4 minutes each side or until browned. Remove from the pan and set aside. Add the remaining oil, leek and garlic to the pan and cook for a further 2–3 minutes or until the leek is tender. Add the tomato paste and cook for a further minute. Add the wine and cook for 1–2 minutes to evaporate. Return the veal to the pan, add the tomato puree, stock, rosemary, bay leaves, salt and pepper and bring to the boil. Reduce the heat to low, cover tightly and cook for 2 hours or until the meat is tender. Add the beans and cook for a further 2 minutes or until heated through. Serves 4.

sirloin steak with red wine sauce

4 x 220g (7¾ oz) sirloin steaks

olive oil, for brushing

sea salt and cracked black pepper

1 quantity red wine sauce (recipe, page 90)

steamed green beans, to serve

watercress leaves, to serve

Pat the steaks dry with absorbent paper. Brush with the oil and sprinkle with the salt and pepper. Heat a large non-stick frying pan over high heat. Add the steaks and cook for 3 minutes or until cooked to your liking. Remove the steak from the pan and keep warm. Serve with the red wine sauce, beans and watercress. Serves 4.

honey mustard beef stir-fry

650g (1 lb 7 oz) rump or topside steak

2 teaspoons vegetable oil

1 clove garlic, crushed

2 onions, cut into wedges

⅓ cup Dijon mustard

¼ cup (60ml/2 fl oz) honey

250g (8 oz) green beans, trimmed

steamed rice, to serve

Trim the steak and cut into slices. Heat a deep non-stick frying pan or wok over high heat until very hot. Add the oil, garlic and onions and cook for 2 minutes. Add the steak strips and cook for 4 minutes or until well browned. Add the mustard, honey and beans and toss to coat. Cook for a further 2–3 minutes or until the beans are just tender. Serve with steamed rice, if desired. Serves 4.

veal with soft polenta and blue cheese

4 x 200g (7 oz) veal cutlets

2 cloves garlic, crushed

¼ cup oregano leaves

2 tablespoons olive oil

sea salt and cracked black pepper

1½ cups (375ml/12 fl oz) chicken stock

1½ cups (375ml/12 fl oz) milk

40g (1½ oz) unsalted butter

1 cup (170g/5⅞ oz) polenta

150g (5¼ oz) blue cheese, sliced

Place the veal, garlic, oregano, oil, salt and pepper in a large bowl and toss to coat. Heat a large non-stick frying pan over medium heat. Add the veal and cook for 5–6 minutes each side. Set aside and keep warm. Place the stock, milk and butter in a medium saucepan over medium heat. Bring to the boil and gradually add the polenta, whisking to combine. Cook for 1 minute, whisking continuously, until thickened. Divide the polenta among serving plates and top with the veal and blue cheese to serve. Serves 4.

veal with soft polenta and blue cheese

chilli jam beef stir-fry

stove-top pie

beef and bean burgers

chilli jam beef stir-fry

6 long mild red chillies, seeds removed
1 tablespoon roughly chopped ginger
1 onion, quartered
3 teaspoons shrimp paste
⅓ cup (60g/2 oz) brown sugar
2 tablespoons vegetable oil
650g (1 lb 7 oz) beef strips
4 green onions (scallions), sliced
200g (7 oz) green beans, trimmed

Place the chillies, ginger, onion, shrimp paste, sugar and oil into a food processor and process until finely chopped. Heat a large non-stick frying pan over high heat and add the chilli paste. Cook, stirring, for 5–7 minutes or until the mixture thickens. Add the beef to the pan and stir-fry for 3 minutes. Add the green onions and beans, cover and cook for a further 3 minutes or until the vegetables are tender. Serves 4.

stove-top pie

1 tablespoon olive oil
1kg (2¼ lb) chuck steak, trimmed and diced
1 brown onion, chopped
2 cloves garlic, crushed
1 tablespoon balsamic vinegar
400g (14 oz) can crushed tomatoes
½ cup (125ml/4 fl oz) beef stock
sea salt and cracked black pepper
1 quantity potato topping (recipe, page 89)

Heat a medium saucepan over high heat. Add the oil and steak and cook in batches for 5 minutes or until well browned. Add the onion and garlic and cook for 2–3 minutes or until the onion is tender. Add the vinegar, tomatoes, stock, salt and pepper. Reduce heat to medium, cover and cook for 20 minutes. Remove the lid and cook for a further 20–25 minutes or until thickened and the meat is soft. Preheat the oven to 200°C (400°F). Spoon the beef mixture into 4 x 1 cup (250ml/8 fl oz) capacity pie dishes. Place the potato topping on top of the pies and bake for 15 minutes or until the potatoes are crisp and golden. Serves 4.

beef and bean burgers

1 quantity cooked beef burgers (recipe, page 88)
½ cup grated mozzarella cheese
½ cup store-bought tomato relish
400g (14 oz) can kidney beans, drained, rinsed and crushed
8 slices Turkish bread, toasted
¼ cup (60g/2 oz) sour cream
1 x 100g (3½ oz) bunch rocket (arugula) leaves

Top the beef burgers with the mozzarella and place on a baking tray under a preheated grill for 3 minutes or until the cheese is melted and golden. Combine the beans and tomato relish. To assemble, spread half of the toast slices with sour cream, top with the bean mixture, burgers and rocket and sandwich with the remaining toast. Makes 4.

red wine and beef simmer

1kg (2¼ lb) beef blade steak, chopped
plain (all-purpose) flour, for dusting
¼ cup (60ml/2 fl oz) olive oil
1 brown onion, chopped
4 garlic cloves, crushed
1 cup (250ml/8 fl oz) red wine
2½ cups (625ml/20 fl oz) beef stock
400g (14 oz) can crushed tomatoes
4 bay leaves
4 sprigs thyme
sea salt and cracked black pepper
mashed potato, to serve

Preheat the oven to 180°C (350°F). Place the beef and flour in a bowl and toss to coat, shaking off any excess. Heat 2 tablespoons of the oil in a large ovenproof frying pan over high heat. Add the meat and cook for 3–4 minutes or until well browned. Remove from the pan and set aside. Add the remaining oil to the pan and add the onion and garlic. Cook for 3 minutes or until golden. Gradually add the wine and cook for 2–3 minutes or until reduced by half. Add the beef back to the pan and add the stock, tomatoes, bay leaves, thyme, salt and pepper. Bring to the boil, cover tightly and cook in the oven for 1½ hours or until the beef is tender. Serve with potato mash, if desired. Serves 4.

red wine and beef simmer

mozzarella veal with roast tomato salad

spaghetti bolognese

pepper steak sandwich

mozzarella veal with roast tomato salad

8 x 60g (2 oz) flattened veal steaks
sea salt and cracked black pepper
8 sage leaves
4 slices (100g/3½ oz) smoked mozzarella cheese, halved
8 slices prosciutto
60g (2 oz) unsalted butter
2 tablespoons olive oil
1 quantity roast tomato salad (recipe, page 90)

Sprinkle the veal with salt and pepper and top each steak with a sage leaf and a slice of mozzarella. Fold in half and wrap in a slice of prosciutto. Heat a large non-stick frying pan over high heat. Add the butter and oil and cook the veal for 2–3 minutes each side or until cooked through. Serve with the roast tomato salad. Serves 4.

spaghetti bolognese

2 tablespoons olive oil
1 brown onion, chopped
2 cloves garlic, crushed
1kg (2¼ lb) beef mince
⅓ cup tomato paste
2 x 400g (14 oz) cans chopped tomatoes
2 cups (500ml/16 fl oz) beef stock
1 bay leaf
sea salt and cracked black pepper
400g (14 oz) spaghetti
flat-leaf parsley leaves, to serve
shaved parmesan cheese, to serve

Heat a large, deep frying pan over high heat. Add the oil, onion and garlic and cook for 1 minute or until the onion is soft. Add the mince and cook for 5 minutes, breaking up any lumps with a wooden spoon. Add the tomato paste and cook, stirring to combine. Add the tomatoes, stock, bay leaf, salt and pepper and stir to combine. Bring to the boil, reduce the heat to low and simmer for 1 hour or until the sauce is thickened. Cook the pasta in a large saucepan of salted boiling water for 10–12 minutes or until al dente. Drain and divide the pasta among bowls. Top with the sauce, parsley and parmesan. Serves 4.

pepper steak sandwich

8 slices pancetta
250g (8 oz) haloumi cheese, sliced
olive oil, for brushing
4 x 120g (3⅞ oz) very thin beef steaks
sea salt
1 teaspoon cracked black pepper
1 quantity rocket mayonnaise (recipe, page 90)
1 sourdough baguette, quartered and halved lengthways
2 tomatoes, sliced
rocket (arugula) leaves, to serve

Heat a large non-stick frying pan over medium heat. Add the pancetta and cook for 1 minute each side. Set aside. Brush the haloumi with oil and cook for 1–2 minutes each side or until golden. Set aside. Brush the steaks with oil, sprinkle with the salt and pepper and cook for 1–2 minutes each side or until cooked to your liking. To assemble, spread the rocket mayonnaise onto the bread and top with the steak, pancetta, haloumi, tomatoes and rocket, if desired. Serves 4.

prosciutto beef with caramelised onions

1 x 800g (1¾ lb) beef fillet, trimmed
olive oil, for brushing
sea salt and cracked black pepper
12 slices prosciutto
1 quantity caramelised onions (recipe, page 88)

Preheat the oven to 220°C (430°F). Brush the beef with the oil. Sprinkle a piece of non-stick baking paper with the salt and pepper and roll the beef on the paper to coat. Heat a large non-stick frying pan over high heat. Cook the beef for 4–5 minutes, turning to brown all sides. Place the overlapping prosciutto slices on a board so they are the same length as the beef, top with the caramelised onions. Place the beef on one edge of the prosciutto and wrap the prosciutto around it. Secure the prosciutto with kitchen string. Place the beef on a rack in a baking dish. Roast for 15 minutes. Reduce the temperature to 180°C (350°F) and roast for a further 5 minutes for rare, or until cooked to your liking. Remove from the oven, cover and rest for 10 minutes before slicing. Serves 4.

prosciutto beef with caramelised onions

coconut red beef curry

carpaccio with crispy capers and spinach

Thai basil and beef salad

coconut red beef curry

500g (1 lb) beef eye fillet
4 tablespoons red curry paste (recipe, page 90)
2 tablespoons vegetable oil
1½ cups (375ml/12 fl oz) coconut cream
¾ cup (185ml/6 fl oz) chicken stock
sea salt and cracked black pepper
200g (7 oz) green beans, trimmed and steamed

Preheat the oven to 180°C (350°F). Brush the beef with half the curry paste. Heat a large non-stick frying pan over high heat. Add 1 tablespoon of the oil and cook the beef for 2–3 minutes each side or until browned. Place the beef on a baking tray and cook for 8–10 minutes for medium–rare or until cooked to your liking. Cover and set aside. Heat the frying pan over medium heat, add the remaining oil and curry paste and cook for 1–2 minutes. Stir in the coconut cream and stock and simmer for 3–4 minutes or until slightly thickened. Slice the beef, place on a serving plates with the beans and spoon the curry sauce over. Serves 4.

carpaccio with crispy capers and spinach

250g (8¾ oz) beef eye fillet
sea salt and cracked black pepper
2 tablespoons olive oil
1 tablespoon salted capers, drained and rinsed
70g (2½ oz) baby spinach leaves
½ cup shaved parmesan cheese, to serve
¼ cup (60ml/2 fl oz) lemon-scented olive oil

Sprinkle the beef with salt and pepper, wrap in plastic wrap and place in the freezer for 1 hour or until just frozen. Heat a non-stick frying pan over high heat. Add the oil and capers and cook for 3–4 minutes or until crispy. Drain and allow to cool.

Using a sharp knife, carefully slice the semi-frozen beef into very thin slices. Divide the beef (carpaccio) among plates and sprinkle over the capers. Top the carpaccio with the spinach and parmesan and drizzle over the lemon oil to serve. Serves 4 as a starter.

Thai basil and beef salad

500g (1 lb) beef eye fillet
olive oil, for brushing
sea salt and cracked black pepper
2 Lebanese cucumbers, thinly sliced
1½ cups Thai basil leaves
1½ cups basil leaves
1 green onion (scallion), finely sliced, to serve
1 red chilli, seeds removed and finely sliced, to serve
1 quantity Thai lime dressing (recipe, page 90)

Preheat the oven to 180°C (350°F). Brush the beef with oil and sprinkle with salt and pepper. Heat a large non-stick frying pan over medium heat. Cook the beef for 3–4 minutes each side or until browned. Place on a baking tray and cook for 12–15 minutes. Set aside to rest for 10 minutes and slice thinly. Layer the beef, cucumber, Thai basil and basil on plates. Top with the green onion and chilli and pour over the Thai lime dressing to serve. Serves 4.

steak with cannellini bean mash and rosemary oil

1.25kg (2¾ lb) potatoes, peeled and chopped
½ cup (125ml/4 fl oz) (single or pouring) cream
sea salt and cracked black pepper
400g (14 oz) can cannellini (white) beans, drained and rinsed
4 x 150g (5¼ oz) beef eye fillet steaks
olive oil, for brushing
1 quantity rosemary oil (recipe, page 90)

Cook the potatoes in a large saucepan of boiling water until soft. Drain, return to the pan and mash with the cream, salt and pepper. Return the saucepan to a low heat, fold in the cannellini beans and mash roughly with a fork. Set aside and keep warm. Heat a medium non-stick frying pan over medium–high heat. Brush the steaks with olive oil and sprinkle with salt and pepper. Cook for 3 minutes each side or until cooked to your liking. To serve, divide the mash among plates, top with the steak and drizzle with the rosemary oil. Serves 4.

steak with cannellini bean mash and rosemary oil

moussaka

4 eggplants (aubergines), sliced

⅓ cup (80ml/2½ fl oz) olive oil

1 brown onion, chopped

3 garlic cloves, crushed

1kg (2¼ lb) beef mince

2 tablespoons tomato paste

2 cups (500ml/16 fl oz) tomato puree

sea salt and cracked black pepper

1.5kg (3¼ lb) fresh ricotta cheese

5 eggs

2 tablespoons thyme leaves

500g (1 lb) starchy potatoes, peeled and sliced

1 cup basil leaves

1 cup oregano leaves

1 cup finely grated parmesan cheese

2 cups grated mozzarella cheese

salad, to serve

Preheat the oven to 200°C (400°F). Brush the eggplant with half the oil and place on baking trays lined with non-stick baking paper. Bake for 10–15 minutes or until golden. Set aside. Reduce the oven to 180°C (350°F). Heat a large saucepan over high heat, add the remaining oil, onion and garlic and cook for 2–3 minutes. Add the mince and cook for 5 minutes or until well browned, breaking up any lumps. Add the tomato paste and cook for 1 minute. Add the tomato puree, salt and pepper, reduce the heat to low and simmer for 15–20 minutes or until the sauce is thickened. Place the ricotta, eggs and thyme in a bowl and mix well to combine. Place the potatoes in a single layer in the base of a 16 cup (4 litre/128 fl oz) capacity ovenproof baking dish. Top with the eggplant and spread with half the ricotta mixture. Top with half the basil and oregano and sprinkle over half the parmesan and mozzarella. Spoon over the mince and top with the remaining herbs. Spread over the remaining ricotta and top with the remaining cheeses. Bake for 40 minutes or until the top is golden. Serve with the salad. Serves 10–12.

classic meat pies

1 quantity shortcrust pastry (recipe, page 89)

375g (13¼ oz) block store-bought puff pastry, thawed

1 egg, lightly beaten

beef filling

1 tablespoon oil

2 onions, chopped

1.5kg (3¼ lb) round or chuck steak, trimmed and diced

1 tablespoon tomato paste

4½ cups (1125 ml/36 fl oz) beef stock

1 cup (250ml/8 fl oz) red wine

1 tablespoon Worcestershire sauce

2 tablespoons cornflour (cornstarch)

¼ cup (60ml/2 fl oz) water

sea salt and cracked black pepper

To make the beef filling, heat the oil in a saucepan over high heat. Add the onion and cook for 2 minutes or until soft. Add the meat and cook for 5 minutes or until sealed. Add the tomato paste, stock, wine and Worcestershire sauce to the pan and simmer, uncovered, for 1 hour or until the meat is tender. Blend the cornflour and water to a smooth paste. Add to the beef mixture and stir for 4 minutes or until the mixture has thickened and returned to a simmer. Add the salt and pepper then set aside to cool.

Preheat the oven to 180°C (350°F). Roll out the shortcrust pastry on a lightly floured surface to 3mm (⅛ in) thick. Cut out six pie bases (you may need to re-roll the scraps) to line pie tins with 9cm (3½ in) diameter bases and 11cm (4½ in) diameter tops. Spoon in the filling. Roll out the puff pastry until 3mm (⅛ in) thick and cut out six lids. Place on top, trim and press the edges of the pastry together. Brush the tops with the egg and make a slit in the tops. Bake for 30 minutes or until golden. Makes 6.

moussaka   classic meat pies

lamb

With its sweet, juicy meat and affinity for both quick and slow cooking methods, it's little wonder that lamb has been the meat of celebration since biblical times. So bring out the barbie or heat up the grill, frying pan or oven and roast, stew, stir-fry and grill your way through this collection of simple yet sensational recipes for festive and everyday occasions.

zaatar lamb with lemon spinach

lamb cutlets with tarragon-potato salad   pan-fried mustard lamb

zaatar lamb with lemon spinach

3 x 200g (7 oz) lamb backstraps (boneless loins), trimmed
1 tablespoon olive oil
1½ tablespoons zaatar (see glossary)
sea salt and cracked black pepper
2 tablespoons olive oil, extra
2 cloves garlic, sliced
400g (14 oz) English spinach leaves, trimmed
1 tablespoon lemon zest
1 tablespoon chopped preserved lemon
500g (1 lb) haloumi cheese, sliced
lemon wedges, to serve

Place the lamb, oil, zaatar, salt and pepper in a bowl and toss to coat. Heat a non-stick frying pan over high heat. Cook the lamb for 3–4 minutes each side or until cooked to your liking. Set aside and keep warm. Add 1 tablespoon of the extra oil, garlic, spinach, zest and preserved lemon. Cook, tossing gently, until the spinach is just wilted. Set aside and keep warm. Heat a large non-stick frying pan over high heat. Add the remaining oil and cook the haloumi slices in batches for 2–3 minutes each side or until golden. Slice the lamb and serve with the spinach, haloumi and lemon wedges, if desired. Serves 4.

lamb cutlets with tarragon-potato salad

8 cutlet lamb rack, trimmed and cut into 4 cutlets
olive oil, for brushing
sea salt and cracked black pepper
1 quantity tarragon-potato salad (recipe, page 90)

Heat a large non-stick frying pan over medium heat. Brush the lamb with the oil and season with the salt and pepper. Cook the lamb for 3–4 minutes each side or until cooked to your liking. Allow to rest. To serve, divide the potato salad among plates and top with the lamb cutlets. Serves 4.

pan-fried mustard lamb

1 tablespoon hot English mustard
3 x 200g (7 oz) lamb backstraps (boneless loins), trimmed
1 tablespoon olive oil
300g (10½ oz) green beans, trimmed and blanched
300g (10½ oz) sugar snap peas, trimmed and blanched
½ cup frozen peas, blanched
2 cups baby rocket (arugula) leaves
1 quantity wine vinegar dressing (recipe, page 91)
hot English mustard, extra, to serve

Spread the mustard over the lamb. Heat a non-stick frying pan over medium–high heat. Add the oil and lamb and cook for 3–4 minutes each side or until cooked to your liking. Rest lamb then slice. Combine the beans, peas, rocket and wine vinegar dressing and serve with the lamb and extra mustard, if desired. Serves 4.

lemon and oregano roast lamb

1 cup (50g/1¾ oz) fresh breadcrumbs
¼ cup chopped oregano leaves
4 anchovy fillets, finely chopped
2 teaspoons finely grated lemon rind
⅓ cup (80ml/2½ fl oz) olive oil
2 cloves garlic, crushed
sea salt and cracked black pepper
800g (1¾ lb) boned lamb shoulder, trimmed
800g (1¾ lb) floury (starchy) potatoes, halved

Preheat the oven to 180°C (350°F). Place the breadcrumbs, oregano, anchovies, lemon rind, 1 tablespoon of the oil, garlic, salt and pepper in a bowl and mix to combine. Place the breadcrumb mixture in the centre of the lamb, roll to enclose the filling and tie with kitchen string to secure. Brush the lamb with 1 tablespoon of the oil and sprinkle with salt and pepper. Heat a large non-stick frying pan over high heat. Cook the lamb for 5 minutes on each side or until well browned. Place the potatoes and the remaining oil in a large baking dish and toss to coat. Top with the lamb, cover with aluminium (aluminum) foil and roast for 1½ hours. Remove the foil and roast for a further 30 minutes or until the lamb and potatoes are cooked through. Serves 4.

lemon and oregano roast lamb

lamb racks with pine nut crust

cucumber, lamb and pea salad

red wine marinated lamb steaks

lamb racks with pine nut crust

½ cup pine nuts
2 cups flat-leaf parsley leaves, chopped
4 cloves garlic, crushed
2 tablespoons sage leaves, chopped
1 tablespoon olive oil
sea salt and cracked black pepper
2 x 8 cutlet lamb racks, trimmed

Preheat the oven to 180°C (350°F). Place the pine nuts on a baking tray and bake for 5 minutes or until golden. Cool slightly then chop. Mix the pine nuts, parsley, garlic, sage, oil, salt and pepper. Coat the lamb with the pine nut mixture. Place the lamb on a rack in a baking dish and cook for 25–30 minutes or until cooked to your liking. Allow to rest then cut each rack in half. Serves 8.

cucumber, lamb and pea salad

2 x 150g (5¼ oz) lamb fillets, trimmed
1 tablespoon lime juice
½ teaspoon chilli powder
1 tablespoon olive oil
sea salt and cracked black pepper
2 cups baby rocket (arugula) leaves
2 Lebanese cucumbers, thinly sliced
1 cup frozen peas, defrosted
lime dressing
¼ cup (60ml/2 fl oz) lime juice
¼ cup (60ml/2 fl oz) olive oil
1 tablespoon brown sugar

To make the lime dressing, place the lime juice, oil and sugar in a large bowl and whisk to combine. Set aside.

Place the lamb, lime juice, chilli, oil, salt and pepper in a bowl and toss to coat. Heat a medium non-stick frying pan over high heat. Add the lamb and cook for 3–4 minutes or until cooked to your liking. Slice the lamb and arrange on plates with the rocket, cucumber and peas. Spoon over lime dressing to serve. Serves 4.

red wine marinated lamb steaks

8 x 150g (5¼ oz) lamb rump steaks
1 quantity red wine marinade (recipe, page 90)
1kg (2¼ lb) floury (starchy) potatoes, peeled and cut into chips
2 tablespoons vegetable oil
1 x 100g (3½ oz) bunch rocket (arugula) leaves, trimmed

Place the lamb in a non-metallic bowl, pour over the red wine marinade, cover and refrigerate for 1 hour. Preheat the oven to 220°C (430°F). Combine the potatoes and oil in a bowl and toss to coat. Place on a baking tray and cook for 30–35 minutes or until crispy. Set aside. Heat a char-grill (broiler) over medium heat. Cook the lamb for 4 minutes each side or until cooked to your liking. Serve with the chips and rocket. Serves 4.

lamb shanks with tomato and rosemary

8 lamb shanks, trimmed
plain (all-purpose) flour, for coating
2 tablespoons olive oil
2 onions, sliced
4 cloves garlic, sliced
1 cup (250ml/8 fl oz) red wine
2½ cups (625ml/20 fl oz) beef stock
400g (14 oz) can crushed tomatoes
1 tablespoon rosemary leaves
2 tablespoons chopped flat-leaf parsley leaves
sea salt and cracked black pepper
mashed potatoes, to serve

Toss the lamb shanks in flour, shaking off any excess. Place half of the oil in a large, deep frying pan over high heat. Add the shanks and brown well. Remove and set aside. Add the remaining oil to the pan and cook the onions and garlic until golden. Return the shanks to the pan. Add the wine, stock, tomatoes and rosemary and bring to the boil. Reduce the heat, cover and simmer for 1 hour. Remove the shanks and continue to simmer the sauce, uncovered, for 10 minutes or until reduced and thickened. Return the shanks to the pan with the parsley, salt and pepper. Serve with mashed potatoes, if desired. Serves 4.

lamb shanks with tomato and rosemary

cumin-crusted lamb with chickpea salad

lamb patties and tomato salad

pesto lamb cutlets with wilted spinach

cumin-crusted lamb with chickpea salad

4 x 150g (5¼ oz) lamb fillets
2 teaspoons cumin seeds
1 tablespoon olive oil
sea salt and cracked black pepper
2 x 400g (14 oz) can chickpeas (garbanzos), drained and rinsed
2 Lebanese cucumbers, thinly sliced
¾ cup mint leaves
50g (1¾ oz) baby spinach leaves
1 quantity yoghurt dressing (recipe, page 91)

Place the lamb, cumin, oil, salt and pepper in a bowl and toss to coat. Heat a large non-stick frying pan over medium heat. Add the lamb and cook for 2–3 minutes each side or until cooked to your liking. Slice the lamb, divide the lamb, chickpeas, cucumber, mint and spinach among plates. Serve with the yoghurt dressing. Serves 4.

lamb patties and tomato salad

500g (1 lb) lamb mince
½ cup (25g/⅞ oz) fresh breadcrumbs
1 red onion, chopped
½ teaspoon ground cumin
1 teaspoon finely chopped rosemary leaves
sea salt and cracked black pepper
4 rashers bacon, trimmed and halved
vegetable oil, for shallow frying
4 tomatoes, sliced
1 cup basil leaves
2 tablespoons balsamic vinegar
2 tablespoons olive oil

Place the mince, breadcrumbs, onion, cumin, rosemary, salt and pepper in a bowl and mix well to combine. Use a ¼ cup (60ml/2 fl oz measure) to divide the mince mixture into eight. Shape into patties and wrap with the bacon. Cover the base of a non-stick frying pan with the oil and heat over medium heat. Add the patties and cook for 3 minutes each side or until cooked through. Place the tomatoes, basil, balsamic and olive oil in a bowl and toss to combine. Serve the salad with the patties and spoon over any remaining balsamic mixture. Serves 4.

pesto lamb cutlets with wilted spinach

8 lamb cutlets, trimmed
2 tablespoons store-bought pesto
100g (3½ oz) baby spinach leaves
100g (3½ oz) fetta cheese, sliced

Heat a large non-stick frying pan over high heat. Brush the lamb with the pesto and cook for 3–4 minutes each side or until cooked to your liking. Add the spinach and cook for 30 seconds or until wilted. Top with the fetta and serve immediately. Serves 4.

minty roasted lamb on potato stacks

1 quantity mint dressing (recipe, page 89)
8 cutlet lamb rack, trimmed
100g (3½ oz) baby spinach leaves, to serve
potato stacks
2 teaspoons olive oil
1 brown onion, thinly sliced
1 tablespoon brown sugar
1 tablespoon balsamic vinegar
3 floury (starchy) potatoes, peeled and thinly sliced
1 cup (250ml/8 fl oz) (single or pouring) cream
1 cup shaved parmesan cheese

To make the potato stacks, preheat the oven to 220°C (430°F). Heat a medium non-stick frying pan over high heat. Add the oil and onion and cook for 2 minutes or until the onion starts to soften. Add the sugar and balsamic and cook for 6 minutes or until the onion is caramelised. Place two layers of potato over the base of a 32 x 21cm (12¾ x 8¼ in) greased baking dish lined with baking paper. Top with a layer of caramelised onion. Repeat with the remaining potato and onion, finish with a layer of potato. Pour over the cream and top with the parmesan. Bake for 30 minutes or until the potato is tender and the top is golden.

Meanwhile, brush ¼ cup (60ml/2 fl oz) of the mint dressing over the lamb. Place the lamb in a baking dish and roast for 20 minutes or until cooked to your liking. To serve, cut the potato stack in four and place on serving plates. Cut the rack into four pieces, place on top of the potatoes and serve with spinach. Spoon over the remaining dressing. Serves 4.

minty roasted lamb on potato stacks

lamb, pea and mint fritters

three-cheese polenta with lamb cutlets

mint and honey-glazed roast lamb

61

lamb, pea and mint fritters

1 cup (150g/5¼ oz) self-raising (self-rising) flour, sifted
2 eggs
20g (¾ oz) butter, melted
⅓ cup (80ml/2½ fl oz) milk
sea salt and cracked black pepper
200g (7 oz) cooked lamb, sliced
¼ cup chopped mint leaves
1 cup frozen peas, defrosted
vegetable oil, for shallow-frying
store-bought tomato relish, to serve

Place the flour, eggs, butter, milk, salt and pepper in a large bowl
and whisk to combine. Fold through the lamb, mint and peas. Place
two tablespoons of oil in a large non-stick frying pan and heat over
medium heat. Add ⅓ cups (80ml/2½ fl oz) of the mixture and cook,
in batches, for 1–2 minutes each side or until lightly browned. Set
aside and keep warm. Add another two tablespoons of oil and repeat
with the remaining mixture. Serve with the tomato relish. Serves 2.

three-cheese polenta with lamb cutlets

8 lamb cutlets, trimmed
olive oil, for brushing
sea salt and cracked black pepper
1 quantity three-cheese polenta (recipe, page 90)
1 x 100g (3½ oz) bunch rocket (arugula) leaves, trimmed

Heat a non-stick frying pan over high heat. Brush the cutlets with oil,
sprinkle with salt and pepper and cook for 4–5 minutes each side or
until cooked to your liking. Set the cutlets aside and keep warm. Divide
the three-cheese polenta among serving plates, top with the cutlets
and rocket to serve. Serves 4.

mint and honey-glazed roast lamb

1 quantity mint and honey glaze (recipe, page 89)
3 x 300g (10½ oz) lamb rump roasts, trimmed
12 baby/chat (new) potatoes, halved
1 tablespoon olive oil

Preheat the oven to 200°C (400°F). Place the mint and honey glaze
in a large non-metallic bowl, add the lamb and toss to coat. Allow
to marinate for 20 minutes.

   Place the potatoes in a metal baking dish with the oil and toss to
coat. Reserving the marinade, place the lamb on a wire rack above
the potatoes and cook for 20 minutes or until the lamb is cooked to
your liking and the potatoes are tender and golden. Place the reserved
marinade in a small saucepan over medium heat and simmer for
2–3 minutes. Serve with the lamb and potatoes. Serves 6.

lamb curry

4 x 150g (5¼ oz) lamb fillets
2 teaspoons ground coriander (cilantro)
2 teaspoons ground cumin
2 tablespoons vegetable oil
2 eschalots, chopped
2 cloves garlic, crushed
1 long red chilli, chopped
2 cups (500ml/16 fl oz) chicken stock
½ cup (55g/1⅞ oz) almond meal (ground almonds)
1 Lebanese cucumber, thinly sliced
chives, to serve

Place the lamb, coriander and cumin in a bowl and toss to coat. Set
aside. Heat a large, deep frying pan over medium heat. Add the oil and
lamb and cook for 2–3 minutes for medium-rare or until cooked to your
liking. Remove the lamb, cover and set aside. Add the eschalots, garlic
and chilli to the pan and cook for 5–6 minutes or until the eschalots are
soft. Gradually add the stock, stirring. Add the almond meal and cook
for 3–4 minutes or until the sauce is thickened. Slice the lamb and
serve with the curry sauce, cucumber and chives. Serves 4.

lamb curry

lamb and mashed potato pie

⅓ cup (80ml/2½ fl oz) olive oil

1kg (2¼ lb) diced lamb

1 brown onion, chopped

2 cloves garlic, crushed

2 tablespoons tomato paste

1 cup (250ml/8 fl oz) red wine

2 cups (500ml/16 fl oz) chicken stock

1 tablespoon chopped rosemary leaves

1kg (2¼ lb) floury (starchy) potatoes, peeled and chopped

80g (2¾ oz) butter

½ cup (125ml/4 fl oz) milk

sea salt and cracked black pepper

¾ cup finely grated parmesan cheese

Heat a large heavy-based saucepan over high heat. Add 2 tablespoons of the oil and cook the lamb in batches for 3–4 minutes or until browned. Set aside.

Add the remaining oil, onion and garlic to the saucepan and cook for 3 minutes or until the onion is softened. Return the lamb to the saucepan, add the tomato paste and cook for 1 minute. Stir in the wine, stock and rosemary and bring to the boil. Reduce the heat to low, cover with a tight-fitting lid and simmer for 1 hour. Remove the lid and simmer for a further 30 minutes or until the lamb is tender. Set aside and keep warm.

Place the potatoes in a large saucepan of salted cold water. Bring to the boil and cook for 15 minutes or until tender when tested with a skewer. Drain and return to the saucepan. Add the butter, milk, salt and pepper and mash until smooth. Set aside.

Divide the lamb mixture between 4 x 1½ cup (375ml/12 fl oz) capacity ovenproof dishes. Top with the mashed potato and parmesan and cook under a preheated hot grill (broiler) for 3–5 minutes or until the top is golden. Makes 4.

lamb with eggplant and yoghurt

300g (10¼ oz) lean lamb mince

1 teaspoon dried oregano leaves

sea salt and cracked black pepper

2 teaspoons red wine vinegar

1 clove garlic, crushed

1 egg yolk

2 Lebanese cucumbers

¼ cup mint leaves

¾ cup (190g/6¾ oz) natural yoghurt

1 tablespoon chopped mint leaves, extra

1 green onion (scallion), sliced

1 x 500g (1 lb) eggplant (aubergine)

olive oil, for brushing

pita bread, to serve

Preheat a barbecue or char-grill (broiler) to medium. Mix the lamb, oregano, salt, pepper, vinegar, garlic and egg yolk. Divide the mixture into four and shape into patties.

To make the cucumber salad, use a vegetable peeler to peel one and a half of the cucumbers into thin ribbons and toss with the mint leaves.

To make the yoghurt dip, chop the remaining cucumber and combine with the yoghurt, extra mint and green onion.

Slice the eggplant into thick slices. Brush the eggplant and lamb patties with oil. Cook the lamb patties and eggplant for 4–5 minutes each side or until cooked to your liking. Serve with the cucumber salad, yoghurt dip and pita bread, if desired. Serves 2.

lamb and mashed potato pie   lamb with eggplant and yoghurt

pork

It could be argued that the world's most widely eaten meat is also the most adaptable. It rises to the occasion in soups, salads and stir-fries and is a natural on the grill or barbecue. But when roasted, pork approaches culinary nirvana – the amazing texture and flavour experience of crispy crackling enclosing meltingly tender leg, loin or belly is almost too good to be legal.

fennel, chilli and rosemary roast pork

chilli-caramelised pork on cucumber salad   pea, pancetta, leek and onion frittata

fennel, chilli and rosemary roast pork

1kg (2¼ lb) pork rack (8 cutlets)
olive oil, for rubbing
3 teaspoons fennel seeds
3 dried chillies
3 teaspoons sea salt flakes
2 tablespoons rosemary leaves
4 brown pears, halved

Preheat the oven to 220°C (430°F). Pat the pork rack dry with absorbent paper. Use the point of a small, sharp knife to score the skin into thin strips and rub the skin with oil. Place the fennel, chillies, salt and rosemary in a small frying pan over medium heat. Cook for 1–2 minutes or until aromatic. Place the fennel salt in the bowl of a small food processor and process until crushed. Rub the fennel salt over the pork rack and cut the rack into four double cutlets. Place the cutlets on a wire rack in a metal baking dish and roast for 25 minutes. Reduce the heat to 200°C (400°F). Add the pears to the bottom of the baking dish and cook for a further 10–12 minutes or until the pork is cooked to your liking and the pears are tender. Serves 4.

chilli-caramelised pork on cucumber salad

1 tablespoon sesame oil
3 x 250g (8 oz) pork fillets, trimmed and sliced
1 tablespoon grated ginger
1 long mild red chilli, seeded and chopped
¼ cup (60ml/2 fl oz) soy sauce
⅔ cup (125g/4 oz) brown sugar
1 tablespoon fish sauce
2 tablespoons lime juice
1 quantity cucumber salad (recipe, page 89)

Heat the oil in a large non-stick frying pan or wok over high heat. Add the pork and cook for 2 minutes each side or until just cooked through. Remove pork and set aside. Reduce the heat to low and add the ginger, chilli, soy, sugar, fish sauce and lime juice to the pan. Stir to dissolve the sugar and then simmer for 8 minutes or until thickened. Add the pork and toss in the sauce to coat. Serve with the cucumber salad. Serves 4.

pea, pancetta, leek and onion frittata

20g (¾ oz) unsalted butter
2 teaspoons olive oil
1 brown onion, sliced
1 leek, sliced
6 eggs
1 cup (250ml/8 fl oz) (single or pouring) cream
⅓ cup finely grated parmesan cheese
200g (7 oz) fresh ricotta cheese
1 cup frozen peas, defrosted
5 slices pancetta, halved
baby spinach leaves, to serve

Heat a 22cm (8½ in) frying pan over medium heat. Add the butter and oil and swirl around the pan to coat. Add the onion and leek and cook, stirring, for 5 minutes or until soft. Place the eggs, cream and parmesan in a bowl and whisk to combine. Reduce the heat to low, pour over the egg mixture and cook for 5 minutes or until the edges just start to set. Top with the ricotta, peas and pancetta and cook for 15 minutes or until the egg is almost set. Place under a preheated hot grill (broiler) for 5 minutes or until the egg is set and the top is golden. Serve with spinach, if desired. Serves 4.

sticky Asian pork belly

4 cloves garlic, crushed
2 teaspoons finely grated ginger
¼ cup (60ml/2 fl oz) hoisin sauce
1 cup (250ml/8 fl oz) Chinese cooking wine or sherry
¼ cup (45g/1⅔ oz) brown sugar
2 tablespoons kecap manis (see glossary)
1 cup (250ml/8 fl oz) water
1kg (2¼ lb) pork belly

Combine the garlic, ginger, hoisin, wine, sugar, kecap manis and water in a bowl. Place the pork belly, skin side down, in a baking dish, pour over the marinade, cover and refrigerate for 1 hour. Preheat the oven to 180°C (350°F). Cover the dish with aluminium (aluminum) foil and roast for 2 hours, remove the foil and roast for a further 30 minutes or until the pork is cooked and the marinade is sticky. Serves 6.

sticky Asian pork belly

plum-glazed pork with snow peas

Asian-style pork ribs

thyme-crusted pork schnitzel

plum-glazed pork with snow peas

1 tablespoon vegetable oil
1 brown onion, sliced
3 x 250g (8 oz) pork fillets, trimmed and sliced
1 teaspoon grated ginger
1 clove garlic, crushed
¼ cup (60ml/2 fl oz) chicken stock
⅓ cup plum jam
1 tablespoon soy sauce
¼ teaspoon Chinese five-spice powder
200g (7 oz) snow peas (mange tout), trimmed and halved
steamed rice, to serve

Heat the oil in a wok or large non-stick frying pan over high heat. Place
the onion in the pan and cook for 2 minutes. Add the pork and cook
in batches for 3 minutes. Remove the onion and pork and set aside.
Add the ginger, garlic, stock, jam, soy and five-spice to the pan and
cook, stirring, for 1–2 minutes or until the jam is melted. Return the
pork and onion to the pan, add the snow peas and cook for 1 minute
or until the snow peas are tender. Serve with steamed rice. Serves 4.

Asian-style pork ribs

1.5kg (3¼ lb) or 16 American-style pork spare ribs
hoisin marinade
½ cup (125ml/4 fl oz) hoisin sauce
1 tablespoon grated ginger
¼ cup (60ml/2 fl oz) soy sauce
2 teaspoons sesame oil
½ cup (125ml/4 fl oz) Chinese rice wine or sherry
1 teaspoon Chinese five-spice powder
2 tablespoons sugar

Preheat the oven to 180°C (350°F). Cut the ribs into individual pieces.
To make the marinade, combine all the ingredients in a large bowl. Add
the ribs and toss to coat. Reserve the remaining marinade to brush over
the ribs while cooking. Place the ribs on a wire rack in a baking dish.
Bake for 20 minutes, then brush with the reserved marinade. Bake for
a further 20 minutes or until well browned. Serves 4.

thyme-crusted pork schnitzel

1 tablespoon thyme leaves
2 tablespoons chopped flat-leaf parsley leaves
1¼ cups (60g/2 oz) fresh breadcrumbs
sea salt and cracked black pepper
4 x 180g (6¼ oz) pork steaks
1 tablespoon hot English mustard
vegetable oil, for shallow-frying
300g (10½ oz) green beans, trimmed and blanched
lemon wedges, to serve
1 quantity horseradish mayonnaise (recipe, page 89)

Place the thyme, parsley, breadcrumbs, salt and pepper in a bowl and
stir to combine. Brush the pork with mustard and press into the thyme
mixture. Heat 1cm (½ in) of oil in a large non-stick frying pan over
medium heat. Add the pork and cook in batches for 2 minutes each
side or until golden and cooked through. Serve with the beans, lemon
and horseradish mayonnaise. Serves 4.

lemon pork and roasted vegies

2 x 250g (8 oz) pork fillets, trimmed and halved
olive oil, for brushing
8 slices pancetta
4 sprigs lemon thyme
400g (14 oz) kipfler potatoes, halved
4 unpeeled cloves garlic
2 tablespoons olive oil, extra
sea salt and cracked black pepper
1 x 250g (8 oz) punnet truss cherry tomatoes

Preheat the oven to 200°C (400°F). Brush the pork with oil, top with
pancetta and thyme and secure with kitchen string. Set aside. Place
the potatoes, garlic, extra oil, salt and pepper in a baking dish and toss
to coat. Roast for 20 minutes. Add the pork and tomatoes and cook
for a further 20 minutes or until the pork is cooked through and the
potatoes are golden. Serves 4.

lemon pork and roasted vegies

coriander and garlic pork

Chinese barbecue pork

Thai caramelised pork salad

coriander and garlic pork

4 x 180g (6¼ oz) pork cutlets
1 quantity coriander marinade (recipe, page 89)
500g (1 lb) baby/chat (new) potatoes, sliced
2 green onions (scallions), sliced
¼ cup mint leaves, chopped
rocket (arugula) leaves, to serve

Place the pork and half the coriander marinade in a bowl and toss to coat. Allow to stand for 10 minutes.

Place the potatoes in a large saucepan of salted cold water. Bring to the boil and cook for 10–12 minutes or until tender when tested with a skewer. Drain and return to the saucepan. Add the remaining coriander marinade, mint and green onions and toss to combine. Set aside and keep warm. Heat a large non-stick frying pan over medium heat. Add the pork, cover with a tight-fitting lid and cook for 3–4 minutes each side or until cooked to your liking. Serve with the potatoes and rocket. Serves 4.

Chinese barbecue pork

¼ cup (60ml/2 fl oz) hoisin sauce
2 tablespoons soy sauce
¼ cup (60ml/2 fl oz) honey
1½ tablespoons Chinese cooking wine or dry sherry
1 teaspoon Chinese five-spice powder
1kg (2¼ lb) pork neck cut into strips 5cm (2 in) wide
steamed rice, to serve
steamed Asian greens, to serve

Combine the hoisin, soy, honey, wine and five-spice in a non-metallic bowl. Add the pork pieces and mix to coat well. Cover and refrigerate for at least 3 hours or overnight.

Preheat the oven to 200°C (400°F). Drain the pork, reserving the marinade, and place on a rack in a baking dish. Bake for 40 minutes or until cooked through, brushing frequently with the marinade. Slice the pork and serve with steamed Asian greens and rice. Serves 4.

Thai caramelised pork salad

¼ cup (60ml/2 fl oz) soy sauce
¼ cup (55g/1⅞ oz) caster (superfine) sugar
2 small red chillies, seeded and chopped
1 tablespoon shredded ginger
2 tablespoons fish sauce
2 tablespoons lime juice
1 teaspoon ground star anise
3 x 250g (8 oz) pork fillets, trimmed
mixed herb salad
100g (3½ oz) salad leaves
4 green onions (scallions), sliced
¼ cup basil leaves
¼ cup mint leaves
¼ cup coriander (cilantro) leaves

Place the soy, sugar, chillies, ginger, fish sauce, lime juice and star anise in a deep frying pan over medium heat and cook, stirring, for 4–5 minutes or until the mixture thickens slightly. Halve the pork fillets lengthways and add to the pan. Cook for 4 minutes on each side or until tender. Remove the pork from the pan and cool slightly. Simmer the pan juices until thickened.

To make the salad, toss together the salad leaves, green onions, basil, mint and coriander. Slice the pork, drizzle with the pan juices and serve with the salad. Serves 4.

chorizo and herb chickpea salad

¼ cup (60ml/2 fl oz) olive oil
4 x 100g (3½ oz) chorizo sausages, sliced
2 x 400g (14 oz) cans chickpeas (garbanzos), drained and rinsed
2 cups cooked couscous
½ teaspoon chilli flakes
1 cup mint leaves
1 red onion, sliced

Heat a large non-stick frying pan over high heat. Add 2 teaspoons of the oil and the chorizo and cook for 3–4 minutes or until browned. Drain on absorbent paper. Combine the chorizo, chickpeas, couscous, chilli, mint, onion and the remaining oil in a bowl. Serves 4.

chorizo and herb chickpea salad

Chinese soup with pork dumplings

roast pork loin with pear and sage

caramelised onions with mustard pork

Chinese soup with pork dumplings

600g (1¼ lb) minced pork
⅓ cup (80ml/2½ fl oz) hoisin sauce
1 tablespoon grated fresh ginger
2 egg whites
⅓ cup chopped fresh coriander (cilantro) leaves
8 cups (2 litres/64 fl oz) chicken stock
2 star anise
1 cinnamon stick
2 tablespoons soy sauce
400g (14 oz) gai larn (Chinese broccoli), chopped
2 finely sliced green onions (scallions)

Combine the pork, hoisin, ginger, egg whites and coriander in a bowl. Roll the mixture into small balls and chill in the fridge.

Heat the chicken stock, star anise, cinnamon stick and soy sauce in a saucepan over medium–high heat and simmer for 2 minutes. Add the dumplings and cook for 4 minutes. Add the gai larn and cook for a further 2 minutes. To serve, place the warm dumplings in bowls, pour over the soup and top with green onion. Serves 4.

roast pork loin with pear and sage

1 brown pear, sliced
2 tablespoons chopped sage
1 tablespoon brown sugar
15g (½ oz) butter, softened
sea salt and cracked black pepper
3kg (6¾ lb) boneless loin of pork (or 2.5kg/5 lb, trimmed)
olive oil, for rubbing

Place the pear, sage, sugar, butter, salt and pepper in a bowl and toss to combine. Preheat the oven to 220°C (430°F). With the point of a sharp knife, score the skin of the pork at 1½cm (⅔ in) intervals. Use the knife to separate the skin from the loin, leaving 3cm (1¼ in) joined. Place the coated pears down the middle. Roll the skin over and secure with kitchen string (see page 18). Rub the skin with oil and salt. Place the meat on a rack in a baking dish. Bake for 20 minutes. Reduce the heat to 200°C (400°F) and bake for 50–55 minutes or until the pork is cooked to your liking. Rest before slicing. Serves 8.

caramelised onions with mustard pork

3 brown onions, quartered
4 brown pears, halved
3 bay leaves
½ cup (125ml/4 fl oz) maple syrup
sea salt and cracked black pepper
4 x 200g (7 oz) pork cutlets, trimmed
2 tablespoons olive oil
2 teaspoons thyme leaves
2 teaspoons Dijon mustard
½ teaspoon chilli flakes

Preheat the oven to 200°C (400°F). Place the onions, pears, bay leaves, maple syrup, salt and pepper in a baking dish and toss to coat. Roast for 40–45 minutes or until golden and caramelised.

Place the pork, oil, thyme, mustard and chilli in a bowl and toss to coat. Heat a large non-stick frying pan over medium heat. Add the pork and cook for 4 minutes each side or until cooked through. Serve with caramelised onions and pears. Serves 4.

rosemary pork with garlic-chilli potatoes

2 x 250g (8 oz) pork fillets, trimmed and halved
1 teaspoon chopped rosemary leaves
2 tablespoons olive oil
2 tablespoons lemon juice
1 teaspoon grated lemon rind
sea salt and cracked black pepper
1 quantity garlic-chilli potatoes (recipe, page 89)
300g (10½ oz) green beans, blanched

Place the pork between two sheets of baking paper and flatten (using a meat mallet or rolling pin) to a thickness of 1cm (½ in). Place the pork, rosemary, oil, juice, rind, salt and pepper in a bowl, toss to coat and stand for 2–3 minutes. Heat a non-stick frying pan over high heat. Add the pork and cook for 2 minutes each side or until cooked through. Serve with the garlic-chilli potatoes and beans. Serves 4.

rosemary pork with garlic-chilli potatoes

pepper pork and celery salad

1kg (2¼ lb) baby/chat (new) potatoes
1 tablespoon vegetable oil
3 x 250g (8 oz) pork fillets, trimmed
2 tablespoons olive oil
sea salt and cracked black pepper
2 celery sticks, shaved
150g (5¼ oz) baby spinach leaves
sour cream dressing
½ cup (125g/4 oz) sour cream
1 tablespoon wholegrain mustard
2 teaspoons white wine vinegar
1 clove garlic, crushed
½ cup chopped flat-leaf parsley leaves
¼ cup (60ml/2 fl oz) water

Preheat the oven to 200°C (400°F). To make the sour cream dressing, place the sour cream, mustard, vinegar, garlic, parsley and water in a bowl and stir to combine.

Place the potatoes and vegetable oil in a baking dish, toss to coat and roast for 45 minutes until golden. Towards the end of cooking time, heat a non-stick frying pan over high heat. Brush the pork with olive oil, salt and pepper and cook for 1 minute each side. Place the pork on a baking tray and cook in the oven for 10 minutes or until cooked through. Slice the pork. Toss the potatoes, celery, spinach and half the dressing to coat, divide the potato salad and pork among plates and spoon over the remaining dressing to serve. Serves 4.

pork fillet with mixed herb couscous

1½ cups couscous
1½ cups (375ml/12 fl oz) hot chicken stock
1 cup mint leaves
1 cup coriander (cilantro) leaves
½ cup slivered almonds, roasted
sea salt and cracked black pepper
3 x 250g (8 oz) pork fillets, trimmed
1 tablespoon olive oil
1 teaspoon ground cumin
1 tablespoon ground coriander (cilantro)
½ teaspoon paprika
natural yoghurt, to serve

Preheat the oven to 180°C (350°F). Place the couscous in a heatproof bowl and pour over the hot stock. Cover with plastic wrap and allow to stand for 5 minutes or until all the liquid has been absorbed. Stir through the mint, coriander, almonds, salt and pepper. Set aside and keep warm.

Brush the pork with half the oil. Place the cumin, coriander and paprika in a bowl and mix until well combined. Rub the cumin mixture over the pork until well coated. Heat the remaining oil in a large non-stick frying pan over high heat. Cook the pork for 2–3 minutes on each side or until browned. Place on a baking tray and cook in the oven for 15 minutes or until cooked through. Slice the pork and serve with the couscous and yoghurt. Serves 4.

pepper pork and celery salad   pork fillet with mixed herb couscous

*glossary, index
+ conversions*

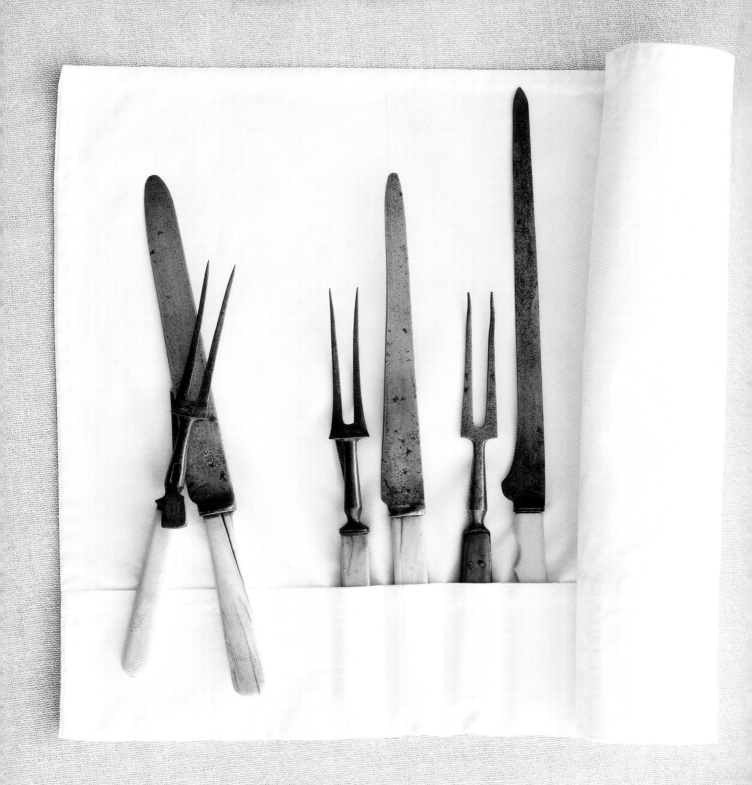

Asian greens

These leafy green vegetables from the brassica family are now becoming widely available. We love their versatility and speed of preparation – they can be poached, braised, steamed or added to soups and stir-fries.

bok choy

A mildly flavoured green vegetable, also known as Chinese chard or Chinese white cabbage. Baby bok choy can be cooked whole after washing. If using the larger type, separate the leaves and trim the white stalks. Limit the cooking time so that it stays green and slightly crisp.

gai larn

Also known as Chinese broccoli or Chinese kale, gai larn is a leafy vegetable with dark green leaves, small white flowers and stout stems (the part of the plant that is most often eaten). Wash thoroughly then steam, braise, boil or stir-fry.

balsamic vinegar

A rich, dark colour and a sweet, mellow, almost caramel flavour distinguish balsamic from other wine vinegars. Made from trebbiano grapes in Modena, Italy, it is aged for 5 to 30 years, or more. The older the balsamic, the better (and more expensive) and the less you'll need to use. Cheaper ones may need to be balanced with some sugar. It should not be used as a substitute for regular vinegar.

beef burgers

250g (8 oz) beef mince
1 teaspoon chilli powder
1 small brown onion, chopped
1 clove garlic, crushed
sea salt and cracked black pepper

Place the mince, chilli, onion, garlic, salt and pepper in a bowl and mix well to combine. Use slightly damp hands to shape the mixture into 4 burgers. Heat a large non-stick frying pan over medium heat and cook for 3 minutes each side or until the burgers are cooked through.

caramelised onions

2 teaspoons olive oil
2 brown onions, sliced
1 tablespoon brown sugar
1 tablespoon balsamic vinegar

Heat a non-stick frying pan over high heat. Add the oil and onions and cook for 3–4 minutes or until the onions are tender. Reduce the heat to low, add the brown sugar and balsamic vinegar and cook, stirring occasionally, for 10 minutes, or until the onions are caramelised.

cheese

A nutritious food made by curdling the milk of cows, goats, sheep and other mammals using rennet and acidic cultures. Some cheeses have moulds on the outer rind or throughout the whole product.

blue cheese

The distinctive veins and flavour of blue cheeses are achieved by adding a cultured mould. Most have a crumbly texture and acidic taste, which becomes rounded and more mellow with age.

fetta

A soft white Greek cheese made from goat's, sheep's or cow's milk, fetta is a salty, crumbly cheese, which is often stored in brine to extend its shelf life.

haloumi

Firm white Cypriot cheese made from sheep's milk. It has a stringy texture and is usually sold in brine. Available from delicatessens and some supermarkets. Holds its shape during grilling and frying, so is ideal for kebabs.

mozzarella

Italian in origin, mozzarella is the mild cheese of pizza, lasagne and tomato salads. It's made by cutting and spinning (or stringing) the curd to achieve a smooth, elastic consistency.

parmesan

Italy's favourite hard, granular cheese is made from cow's milk. Parmigiano reggiano is the Rolls Royce variety, made under strict guidelines in the Emilia-Romagna region and aged for an average of 2 years. Grana padano mainly comes from Lombardy. It's aged for 15 months.

ricotta

A creamy, finely grained white cheese. Ricotta means "recooked" in Italian, a reference to the way the cheese is produced by heating the whey left over from making other cheese varieties. It's fresh and creamy and low in fat.

Chinese five-spice powder

This fragrant combination of ground cinnamon, Sichuan pepper, star anise, clove and fennel is available from Asian food stores and most supermarkets.

Chinese rice wine

Similar to dry sherry, Chinese cooking wine is a blend of glutinous rice, millet, a special yeast and the local spring waters of Shaoxing, where it is made, in northern China. It is sold in Asian supermarkets, often labelled "shao hsing" or "shaoxing".

coriander marinade

1 cup chopped coriander (cilantro) leaves
4 cloves garlic, crushed
sea salt and cracked black pepper
⅔ cup (165ml/5 fl oz) olive oil
Place the coriander, garlic, salt, pepper
and oil in a bowl and stir to combine.

couscous

The name given to both the national
dish of Algeria, Tunisia and Morocco
and the tiny grains of flour-coated
semolina that are used to make it.
Available from supermarkets.

cucumber salad

2 cucumbers, thinly sliced
½ cup bean sprouts
½ cup mint leaves
½ cup coriander (cilantro) leaves
Combine the cucumber, bean sprouts,
mint and coriander.

eschalots

A member of the onion family, eschalots
are smaller and have a milder flavour
than brown, red or white onions. A popular
ingredient in Europe, they look like small
brown onions with purple-grey tinged
skins. Asian shallots are smaller again
with pinkish skins and grow in clusters.

garlic-chilli potatoes

500g (1 lb) baby/chat (new) potatoes,
    quartered
2 cloves garlic, crushed
1 small red chilli, seeded and chopped
1 tablespoon olive oil
Preheat the oven to 200°C (400°F).
Place the potatoes, garlic, chilli, and oil
in a bowl and toss to combine. Place the
potatoes on a baking tray and roast for
20 minutes or until golden and crispy.

horseradish mayonnaise

½ cup (125g/4 oz) store-bought
    whole-egg mayonnaise
¼ cup (60g/2 oz) horseradish cream
Place the mayonnaise and horseradish
cream in a bowl and stir to combine.

kecap manis

Sometimes labelled ketjap manis, this is
a very thick and sweet but salty Indonesian
soy sauce used as a condiment or dipping
sauce. Available from Asian food stores.

mint dressing

⅓ cup (80ml/2½ fl oz) store-bought
    mint sauce
⅓ cup wholegrain mustard
2 tablespoons olive oil
sea salt and cracked black pepper
Place the mint sauce, mustard, oil, salt
and pepper in a bowl and mix to combine.

mint and honey glaze

1 tablespoon olive oil
2 tablespoons honey
1 tablespoon white wine vinegar
¼ cup chopped mint leaves
sea salt and cracked black pepper
Combine the oil, honey, vinegar, mint,
salt and pepper.

pastry

Make your own or use one of the many
store-bought varieties.

puff pastry

This pastry is time-consuming and quite
difficult to make, so many cooks opt to
use store-bought puff pastry. It can be
bought in blocks from patisseries or bought
in both block and sheet forms from the
supermarket. You may need to layer several
sheets of puff pastry together.

shortcrust pastry

A savoury or sweet pastry that is available
ready-made in blocks and frozen sheets.
Keep a supply for last-minute pies and
desserts or make your own.

shortcrust pastry recipe

2 cups (300g/10½ oz) plain
    (all-purpose) flour
145g (5 oz) butter
2–3 tablespoons iced water
Process the flour and butter in a food
processor until the mixture resembles fine
breadcrumbs. While the motor is running,
add enough iced water to form a smooth
dough. Knead very lightly then wrap the
dough in plastic wrap and refrigerate for
30 minutes. When ready to use, roll out
on a lightly floured surface to 3mm (⅛ in)
thickness. This recipe makes 350g (12 oz),
sufficient to line up to a 25cm (10 in) pie
dish or tart tin.

polenta

Used extensively in northern Italy, this corn
meal is cooked in simmering water until
it has a porridge-like consistency. In this
form it is enriched with butter or cheese
and served with meat dishes. Otherwise
it is left to cool, cut into squares and either
grilled, fried or baked.

potato topping

2 potatoes, sliced
1 tablespoon olive oil
2 tablespoons finely grated parmesan
    cheese
Toss the potato slices in the olive oil and
parmesan. Use as a topping for pies.

red curry paste

Buy good-quality pastes in jars from Asian
food stores or the supermarket. When

trying a new brand, it is a good idea to add a little at a time to test the heat as the chilli intensity can vary significantly. Otherwise, make your own.

red curry paste recipe

3 small red chillies
3 cloves garlic, peeled
1 stalk lemongrass, chopped
4 green onions (scallions), chopped
1 teaspoon shrimp paste
2 teaspoons brown sugar
3 kaffir lime leaves, sliced
1 teaspoon finely grated lemon rind
1 teaspoon grated ginger
½ teaspoon tamarind concentrate
2–3 tablespoons peanut oil

Place all the ingredients except the oil in the bowl of a small food processor or spice grinder. With the motor running, slowly add the oil and process until you have a smooth paste. Refrigerate in an airtight container for up to 2 weeks. Makes ½ cup.

red wine marinade

½ cup (125ml/4 fl oz) red wine
2 tablespoons brown sugar
3 cloves garlic, roughly chopped
2 tablespoons roughly chopped rosemary
   leaves
½ cup (125ml/4 fl oz) olive oil
sea salt and cracked black pepper

Place the wine, sugar, garlic, rosemary, olive oil, salt and pepper in a bowl and whisk to combine.

red wine sauce

2 tablespoons red wine
1 tablespoon red wine vinegar
1 teaspoon cracked black pepper
¾ cup (185ml/6 fl oz) beef stock

Combine the wine, vinegar and pepper

in a small saucepan and cook over high heat for 1–2 minutes. Add the stock and cook for 3–4 minutes or until the sauce is slightly thickened.

roast tomato salad

500g (1 lb) vine-ripened cherry tomatoes
100g (3½ oz) rocket (arugula) leaves
shaved parmesan cheese, to serve

Preheat the oven to 180°C (350°F). Place the tomatoes in a baking dish lined with non-stick baking paper and roast for 10 minutes or until tender. Remove from oven and combine the roasted tomatoes with the rocket and parmesan.

rocket mayonnaise

½ cup chopped rocket (arugula) leaves
⅔ cup (160g/5½ oz) store-bought
   whole-egg mayonnaise

Place the rocket and mayonnaise in a bowl and stir to combine.

rosemary oil

¼ cup (60ml/2 fl oz) olive oil
1 clove garlic, finely sliced
1 teaspoon rosemary leaves

Cook the oil, garlic and rosemary in a small saucepan over low heat for 3 minutes or until fragrant.

shrimp paste

Also called blachan, this strong-smelling paste is made from salted and fermented dried shrimps pounded with salt. Used in South-East Asian dishes. Keep sealed in the fridge and fry before using. Available from Asian food stores.

tarragon-potato salad

1kg (2¼ lb) baby/chat (new) potatoes
1 cup frozen peas, defrosted
½ cup (125ml/4 fl oz) olive oil

1 tablespoon lemon juice
1 teaspoon finely grated lemon rind
1 long mild green chilli, roughly chopped
1 tablespoon tarragon leaves
80g (2¾ oz) watercress leaves

Place the potatoes in a large saucepan of salted cold water over high heat. Bring to the boil, then reduce the heat to low and simmer for 15–20 minutes or until the potatoes are soft when tested with a skewer. Drain, cool slightly, slice and set aside. Place the peas, oil, lemon juice, rind, chilli and tarragon in a small food processor and process until roughly chopped. Place the pea mixture, potatoes and watercress in a small bowl and gently toss to combine.

Thai basil

Thai basil is a tropical strain of basil and is common in South-East Asian cooking. It has anise overtones to the basil flavour, and has small, dark green leaves with purple stems and flowers. Used like a vegetable, whole leaves are added to Thai curries, stir-fries, salads and soups. Thai basil, sometimes referred to as holy basil, is available from Asian supermarkets and most green grocers.

Thai lime dressing

¼ cup (60ml/2 fl oz) lime juice
1 teaspoon finely grated lime rind
2 tablespoons fish sauce
2 teaspoons brown sugar
1 teaspoon finely grated ginger

Place the lime juice, rind, fish sauce, sugar and ginger in a bowl and stir well.

three-cheese polenta

2 cups (500ml/16 fl oz) hot water
2½ cups (625ml/20 fl oz) milk
1 cup instant polenta

60g (2 oz) butter
1 cup grated cheddar cheese
50g (1¾ oz) soft blue cheese
¼ cup grated parmesan cheese

Place the water and milk in a large
saucepan over high heat and bring to the
boil. Slowly pour in the polenta, whisking
continuously to prevent any lumps from
forming. Reduce the heat to low and stir
with a wooden spoon for 5–6 minutes
or until the polenta starts to leave the
sides of the pan. Stir through the butter,
cheddar, blue cheese and parmesan and
cook for 1 minute.

wine vinegar dressing

2 tablespoons red wine vinegar
2½ tablespoons olive oil

Place the vinegar and oil in a bowl and
whisk to combine.

yoghurt dressing

1 cup (250g/8 oz) natural yoghurt
2 tablespoons lemon juice
sea salt

Place the yoghurt, lemon juice and salt
in a bowl and stir to combine.

zaatar

Zaatar is a Middle Eastern seasoning of
sesame, sumac and dried thyme. Sprinkle
on meat and seafood before roasting,
pan-frying or barbecuing.

conversion chart

1 teaspoon = 5ml
1 Australian tablespoon = 20ml (4 teaspoons)
1 UK tablespoon = 15ml (3 teaspoons/½ fl oz)
1 cup = 250ml (8 fl oz)

liquid conversions

metric	imperial	cups
30ml	1 fl oz	⅛ cup
60ml	2 fl oz	¼ cup
80ml	2½ fl oz	⅓ cup
125ml	4 fl oz	½ cup
185ml	6 fl oz	¾ cup
250ml	8 fl oz	1 cup
375ml	12 fl oz	1½ cups
500ml	16 fl oz	2 cups
600ml	20 fl oz	2½ cups
750ml	24 fl oz	3 cups
1 litre	32 fl oz	4 cups

cup measures

1 cup almond meal	110g	3¾ oz
1 cup plain (all-purpose) flour	150g	5¼ oz
1 cup brown sugar	175g	6 oz
1 cup caster (superfine) sugar	220g	7¾ oz
1 cup white sugar	220g	7¾ oz
1 cup arborio rice, uncooked	220g	7¾ oz
1 cup couscous, uncooked	180g	6¼ oz
1 cup basil leaves	45g	1⅔ oz
1 cup coriander (cilantro) leaves	40g	1½ oz
1 cup mint leaves	35g	1¼ oz
1 cup flat-leaf parsley leaves	40g	1½ oz
1 cup olives	175g	6 oz
1 cup parmesan cheese, finely grated	100g	3½ oz
1 cup green peas, frozen	170g	5⅞ oz

A beautiful collection of clever and simple recipes
from Australia's favourite cookbook author

recipe taken from *simple essentials: fruit*

crushed raspberry tart

375g (13¼ oz) store-bought puff pastry, defrosted
1 egg white, lightly beaten
1 tablespoon caster (superfine) sugar
2 cups (250g/8 oz) raspberries
1 tablespoon icing (confectioner's) sugar, sifted
sour cream filling
1 cup (250g/8 oz) sour cream
¼ cup (60ml/2 fl oz) (single or pouring) cream
⅓ cup (60g/2 oz) brown sugar

Preheat the oven to 200°C (400°F). Roll out the pastry on a lightly
floured surface to 3mm (⅛ in) thickness and trim to a 20cm (8 in)
square. Cut 8 strips measuring 1 x 20cm (½ x 8 in) from the
remaining pastry. Place the pastry square on a baking tray lined with
non-stick baking paper. Brush with the egg white and place half the
strips around the edge to form a border. Brush the borders with the
egg white and place the remaining strips on top. Prick the base with
a fork. Cover and refrigerate for 30 minutes. Sprinkle the pastry with
the caster sugar. Bake for 20 minutes or until golden. To make the sour
cream filling, whisk the sour cream, cream and brown sugar in a bowl
until smooth. Combine half the raspberries with the icing sugar and
crush lightly. Fold in the remaining raspberries. Spread the sour cream
filling over the pastry base and spoon over the raspberries. Serves 6.

donna hay
SIMPLE ESSENTIALS

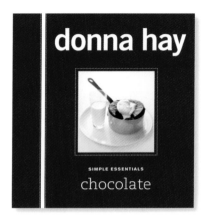

donna hay

SIMPLE ESSENTIALS

chocolate

donna hay

SIMPLE ESSENTIALS

salads + vegetables

donna hay

SIMPLE ESSENTIALS

pasta, rice + noodles

donna hay

SIMPLE ESSENTIALS

chicken

donna hay

SIMPLE ESSENTIALS

fruit

donna hay

SIMPLE ESSENTIALS

beef, lamb + pork

Available now from all booksellers

At the age of eight, Donna Hay put on an apron and
never looked back. She completed formal training in home
economics at technical college then moved to the world
of magazine test kitchens and publishing where she
established her trademark style of simple, smart
and seasonal recipes all beautifully put together and
photographed. It is food for every cook, every food lover,
every day and every occasion. Her unique style turned
her into an international food publishing phenomenon
as a bestselling author, publisher of *donna hay magazine*,
newspaper columnist, and creator of a
homewares and food range.

books by Donna Hay: *off the shelf, modern classics book 1, modern classics
book 2, the instant cook, instant entertaining, simple essentials: chicken,
simple essentials: chocolate, simple essentials: salads + vegetables,
simple essentials: fruit, simple essentials: pasta, rice + noodles,* plus more.